Jan Laurens Siesling

"Say, How Can I Not Miss Her"
Liu Bannong's Ballad

"教我如何不想她"
刘半农的歌谣

Bilingual Edition

Chinese by Haiyan Tian

Just So J!S Editions

Liu Bannong, poet and linguist, was born in 1891 in Jiangyin, a city halfway between Nanjing and Shanghai. He spent his formative years as a writer in post-revolutionary Shanghai. As a professor at the Beijing University and a contributing editor of the progressive magazine New Youth, he became one of the leading figures of the cultural upheaval, known as the 4th of May, in 1919. He studied linguistics in London and Paris, where he obtained a doctoral degree in Phonetics in 1925. In Paris, at the Bibliothèque Nationale, he did groundbreaking research into the Dunhuang monastery manuscripts. He died in 1934 in Beijing.

刘半农，诗人、语言学家，1891年生于江阴，一个位于南京和上海之间的城市。在辛亥革命后的上海度过了他作为一个作家的成长期。作为北京大学的教授和进步杂志《新青年》的特约编辑，他成为1919年五四文化运动的主要人物之一。曾在伦敦和巴黎攻读语言学，于1925年获得语音学博士学位。在巴黎利用国家图书馆，他对敦煌写本进行了开创性研究。他1934年在北京逝世。

Copyright © Just So Editions, October 2020;
© This edition, February 2021
© Chinese edition: The Swallow House, February 2021

ISBN 978-1-5136-6243-5

Qui scribit bis legit

目录　Contents

教我如何不想她	8
Say, how can I not miss her?	9
刘半农的歌谣	12
Liu Bannong's ballad	13
赵元任的曲谱	64
Zhao Yuanren's music scores	65

插图　Illustrations

刘半农肖像	Portrait of Liu Bannong	front cover
刘半农摄影	Photograph by Liu Bannong	back cover
刘半农肖像	Portraits of Liu Bannong	6, 63
赵元仁肖像	Portrait of Zhao Yuanren	62
刘半农摄影	Photographs by Liu Bannong	10, 11

教我如何不想她

刘半农

天上飘着些微云,
地上吹着些微风。
啊!
微风吹动了我头发,
教我如何不想她?

月光恋爱着海洋,
海洋恋爱着月光。
啊!
这般蜜也似的银夜。
教我如何不想她?

水面落花慢慢流,
水底鱼儿慢慢游。
啊!
燕子你说些什么话?
教我如何不想她?

枯树在冷风里摇,
野火在暮色中烧。
啊!
西天还有些儿残霞,
教我如何不想她?

1920 年 9 月 4 日

Say, How Can I Not Miss Her

Light clouds float in the sky,
On earth blows a gentle breeze.
Oh!
Gentle breeze in my waving hair,
Say, how can I not miss her?

Moonlight in love with the ocean,
Ocean in love with the moon.
Oh!
Silver night as honey so sweet,
Say, how can I not miss her?

On water lost flowers flow slow,
In water slow fish swim low.
Oh!
Swallow what words are you singing?
Say, how can I not miss her?

WIthered trees in cold wind shiver,
Wildfire's aflame in the dusk.
Oh!
Last glow over the western sky,
Say, how can I not miss her?

Liu Bannong, September 4, 1920
Translation by Jan L. Siesling, September 4, 2020

刘半农的歌谣

纪念汉语"她"字问世一百周年

—— 给刘育熙

In the evening of the 4th of September 1920, Liu Fu, who also called himself Liu Bannong, signed a short poem, not thinking it would become the most popular Chinese poem of the century [1]. A sequence of four short stanzas of identical format, rhythm and tone, it bears the title *"How can I not miss her"*. This was the line repeated at the end of each quatrain, a refrain. I take the freedom to call it a ballad, a popular English form of verse, not only because the poet, when he wrote it, lived in London and studied English literature, but for the poem's romantic mood, its repetitive structure, its songlike character. The structure is simple, but strict. In each stanza, the first and the last line count seven characters, the two middle lines eight (not leaving out a repeated interjection *Oh!*); together they make up for thirty characters, the number of years of his life the poet had celebrated on May 27, 1920. Most lines present a whole phrase, in a basic format, noun, verb and an adjective or adverb. Every couplet tends toward the last line, presenting a rhetorical question, giving, by its twist of mood, enhanced sense to the foregoing lines. The poem features multiple punctuation marks, as rarely seen in Chinese poems, clearly indicating pauses for breathing; introducing this western custom was since his early youth one of Bannong's recipes for modernizing Chinese, making it more comfortable to read. The use of a quiet rhythm, repetition of words and lines within the couplets, rather than end-rhyme, with accents on words of warm

洪亮的字眼，如此自然悠扬，以致赵元任，这位语言学家、作曲家和诗人的挚友，忍不住为此诗谱上了曲，那是1926年，赵为这首诗谱的曲具有弗朗兹.舒伯特的歌曲特点。上世纪30年代初，这首诗就以歌的形式飞到了每个中国人的心坎上，不管是生活在国内还是国外的，自上世纪三十年代至今日一直在延续。这般受欢迎，在现代诗歌中极为罕见，也赋予了它意义，使得这首诗更值得研究。评论者常倾向于讨论相关的音乐而不是歌词，似乎歌词本身会言说。我这里打算从文字方面来关注这首诗。

不算最近几年或最近几个月的话，我几乎没遇到过这首普世的、如此热门的中文诗的英译本，其后我所见的译本又没有两个是相同的，确实差异很重要[2]。我决定尝试一下。这似乎很容易，错了。简单的中文文本打开了英文里无尽的变数。翻译准确了，但没有诗歌。有诗意了，但不准确。似乎总缺少什么。探索它的起源该会有帮助吧？译和注同步而为。中外学者对这首诗一定有数不尽的解释，但我不知道。以下陈述的内容可能大多以前已被说过了，但我相信几率是其中的一些没被提及过。

———————

sonority, proved so naturally melodious that Zhao Yuanren, linguist and composer and the poet's close friend, couldn't help setting the poem to music in 1926, treating it like a Schubertian Lied. His version reached every Chinese soul, living inside or outside the borders of the country, beginning in the early thirties of the last century, not ceasing until today. It is this popularity, extremely rare for modern poetry, enhancing its meaning, which makes the poem even more worth studying. Reviewers show a tendency to deal with the music rather than the lyrics, as if the words spoke for themselves; I intend to focus on the poem as words.

Without counting the last few years or last few months, I have met with few translations into English of this Chinese top hit of universal inspiration and not two are the same, indeed the differences are important [2]. I decided to try myself. It seemed easy, falsely. The simple Chinese text opens into endless variables in English. Some results are correct, but no poetry; others are poetic, but not correct. Something seems always to be missing. Wouldn't an investigation into its origins be helpful? Translation and interpretation go side by side. There must be numberless interpretations of the poem by Chinese and international scholars, but I don't know them. Much of what follows may have been said before, but I trust chance that some of it is not.

歌谣叙述的主人公是因残酷现实而彼此分离的恋人。乍一看，半农歌词的主题是一位渴望着他心爱女人的诗人。如果用这种方式理解，或者我们继续这样理解，也不是没道理的。但它被分享到全国各地不是因为以上的理解方式；这也不是多数人读它唱它的方式。"她"被理解为中国。让我们先留心一下。那位被隐去姓名、被向往的她一定得大过某个单个的人吗？为什么我们要排除一个隐秘的（而可能是感人的）爱情故事呢，本来又有此诗为线索？嗯，半农已成家了，他妻子跟他在一起，或许他写这首诗时就坐在他的身边。不管在哪儿他一生中似乎没有任何空间可以拥有秘密的激情：他首先是个努力工作的人，不以在酒吧或妓院里消磨时光而得名，他的经济状况也从未充裕到使他金屋藏娇。在历史上遥遥面对我们，他是一个十分忠心和诚实的人。他是一个极其罕见的以履行自我强加的诸多崇高职责来获得满足感的人。他小小年纪就接受了父母给他的包办婚姻，面带微笑地把这种古老传统作为一种优势，他不愿浪费时间在诸如求爱等浅薄的事务上，更不会花时间去玩弄女性，他也没抵制父母的传统观点[3]。不过他拒绝了父亲同样传统的让他纳妾的建议。那些同女人们调情费时的事

Common protagonists of the narrative of a ballad are lovers separated from each other for cruel reasons. And, at first sight, that is the subject of Bannong's lyrics, a poet longing after a woman. We are not unreasonable if we read it that way, nor if we continue to do so. It is not the way that made the poem popular and, consequently, national; not the way the majority now reads it, sings it. *She, her* is understood as China. Let us give it a second of attention. *Must* there be more to *her* than a single, though nameless person longed after? Why should we exclude a hidden (and possibly moving) love story, this poem would be the clue of? Well, Liu Bannong was married, and his wife was with him, maybe sitting next to him when he wrote it. In all his life there seems to have been no room for a secret *passion* anywhere: he was such a hard worker in the first place, not reputed for spending time in bars or brothels, while his financial means had never been sufficient for a hidden *danseuse à Paris* either. He faces us, in the historical distance, as a man of exceptional faithfulness and honesty. He was one of those rare people who draw satisfaction from fulfilling self-imposed noble duties, and these were legion. He had accepted an arranged marriage by his parents at a young age, smilingly taking this antique tradition as an advantage, not willing to lose his time in such shallow business as courting, much less philandering; or countering his parents' traditional views [3]. But he had refused his father's equally traditional suggestion to take a concubine. Those time-consuming things with women,

情，绝对不！事实上他的缺乏浪漫的婚姻似乎是幸福的，某种意义上是患难夫妻、相依为命。伦敦就是这样的时刻。他似乎也总是个有爱心的父亲，当可能的时候；他也是个顾家的人，如果这意味着一个对家庭比常人付出更多的人。于是，他携妻子朱惠和四岁的女儿小惠一起来欧洲冒险。我们这时可以排除未公开的亲密女友是激发"她"诗灵感的可能性了。"她"从他的（伦敦的）家和家人完美地走到了他的家乡江阴的大家庭，再到了每个中国男女都是一员的祖国。这首歌数年后完成了它长长的旅程。我们来仔细回顾一下。

这个小家庭于1920年2月7日乘日本轮船从上海出发，经香港，斯里兰卡，苏伊士，于3月15日在马赛靠岸，从那里再乘火车和渡轮前往伦敦，两天后抵达。对半农来说，这是一次漫长而愉快的旅行，可对于他的妻子而言，这是一次漫长而糟糕的航行，连续晕船，没有人意识到她是怀孕了。
到了英国首都，这个世界上最广阔帝国的首都，第一件要做的事是找个地方住下来。不管是谁一生中曾在伦敦尝试过的都知道这有多难。伦敦是如此之大，即使以中国的标准；随机地延申着它的永无止境的郊区，即使跟中国相比也是如此；又极其昂贵，尤其是对于那时的中国游客。开始它使你兴奋，不久就使你沮丧。还好, 英国人彬彬有礼，乐于助人。

no! In fact, his marriage, for lack of romance, seems to have been happy, in the sense that husband and wife were united in unhappy moments. London was such a moment. He seems to have been a caring father, too, when he could: a family man, if this means a man showing more than usual devotion to his family. Thus, he had taken his wife, Zhu Hui, and four-year-old daughter, Xiao Hui, with him in his European adventure. We drop the possibility of an undisclosed intimate friend as the poem's inspiration. *"She"*, or *"her"* moves seamlessly from his home and family (in London), to his broader family in hometown Jiangyin, and from there to the home country, where every Chinese woman and man can join in. A long trip, it took a few years to complete. Let us take a closer look.

The little family had embarked on February 7, 1920, in Shanghai on a Japanese steamer, and via Hong Kong, Sri Lanka, Suez, disembarked in Marseille, March 15, and from there by train and ferry to London, where they arrived two days later. A long and pleasant trip for Bannong, a long and execrable voyage for his wife, continuously seasick, no one realizing she was pregnant. The first thing to do in the British capital, capital of the world's vastest-ever Empire, was to find a place to live. Whoever in his life has tried this, in London, knows how hard that is. London is so big, even for Chinese standards, spreading its never-ending suburbs so randomly, even compared to China, and so expensive, especially for Chinese visitors in 1920. It excites you in the beginning, will depress you soon after. But British people are polite

半农在西南部布里克斯顿的一条红砖长街上找到了一所令人愉悦的红砖房公寓，住室在一楼（地下室？），该公寓有个诱人的名字叫克兰沃思花园，距市中心有点儿远，每月收合理的15英镑租金。一个昂贵而充满希望的开始。

接下来要做的是在伦敦大学注册，该大学距离市中心同布里克斯顿距离市中心一样的远，不过一个在东北，一个在西南。4月2日，半农迈上注册大楼的台阶，在这里他将申请于学年度的第三学期入学[4]，他注册了四门课，意在更加完善地学习语言。

为这个时刻，他很早以前就已在中国作准备了。半农自1917年一直是北京大学的教授，负责教授汉语语法基础课程。他是一位出色而受人尊敬的老师，他根据自己的经验为他的学生出版了一本语法教科书，该教材在那时已广为流传。校长蔡元培委任他各种职务，如成立一个（教授们的！）进德会，以及在北大创立据点来收集中国民间歌曲和民间诗歌。民歌是半农多年来热衷的事情之一，它们既是语言的瑰宝，又具有古典诗歌所忽视的传统魅力。蔡和刘经常见面，在讨论国家第一所现代大学里的研究状况时，他们能理解彼此。当后者表达了他的愿望，

and helpful. Bannong finds an apartment on the first floor (the basement?) of a gay redbrick house in a long redbrick street in Brixton, S.W., with the enticing name of Cranworth Gardens, a little far from the center, for a reasonable 15 pounds per month. Expensive but hopeful beginnings.

Next thing to do is register at the University of London, situated as much northeast of the center, as Brixton is southwest of it. On April 2, Bannong walks up the stairs leading into the building to apply for entrance to the school in the third term [4], enrolling in four classes, intended to learn the language more perfectly.

This moment had been prepared since long, in China. Liu Bannong, alias Liu Fu, had been a professor at the Peking University since 1917, in charge of teaching foundation classes of Chinese grammar. He was a consummated and appreciated teacher, had even published a grammar textbook for his students, based on his experience, which was already widely distributed. He had been entrusted with various other duties by the President Cai Yuanpei, like putting in place a committee of good morality (of the professors!) as well as the founding of a University Collection of Chinese folk songs and folk poetry. Folk songs had been one of Bannong's passions since years, both as linguistic treasures and for the charm of a tradition neglected by classical poetry. Cai and Liu met often, understood each other when they discussed the state of research in the first modern university of the country. And when the latter had expressed his desire,

或者更确切地是，对汉语语言史进行深远研究的必要性，而开始这一研究只能想象是在欧洲实现，校长于是鼓励他申请去伦敦，这是一个蔡校长自己很了解的城市。可是1919年5月、6月学生反抗运动日趋激烈，对于实施人员特殊待遇来说，这是不太可能的一年。求学被推迟到1920年春，手续才办妥了。教育部批准并提供教授每月20英镑的津贴。外加大学方面的40英镑。应该是够了。

现在刘复，在这儿他所用的名字，站在世界最大的大学的注册办公室里。行政步骤有着它们自己的情绪分量。在朴素的登记表跟前，现实已证明它比梦想复杂得多。半农在"教程"一栏填写的是"语音和艺术"，但他必须（或被建议）注册显然更为适度的"听力训练"、"发音"和"口语英语"等课程。这听起来是很合理的。他的书面英语程度虽然很好，但是英语口语，在英格兰，是另一杯茶。让我们也设想他认为英语的口语同中文的白话相当，他是一位杰出的白话捍卫者，他也一直在诗歌中使用白话。

or rather the necessity, of doing far-reaching research in the linguistic history of the Chinese language, the beginning of which could only be imagined in Europe, the President had encouraged him to apply for a stay in London, a city he knew well himself. 1919, with the student revolt raging in May and June, was the wrong year for personnel to implement extraordinary treatment. It was postponed to the spring of 1920, with success. The Ministry of Education gave its consent and shared in the professor's monthly stipend, 20 pounds sterling. The university added 40. It should be enough.

Now Liu Fu, as he calls himself here, stands in the registrar's office of the biggest university of the world. Administrative steps have an emotional weight of their own. In front of the unassuming registration form, reality proved already more complex than the dream. Bannong indicates as *"course of study"* Phonetics and Arts, but he will (and is probably advised to) enroll in classes of apparently more modest *exercises* of "Ear-Training", of "Pronunciation" and of lectures in "Colloquial English". This sounds reasonable. His level of written English was good, but spoken English, in England, is another cup of tea. Let us also suppose that he expected Colloquial Language to be the equivalent in English of *baihua* in Chinese, he was such a prominent defender of, practicing it in his poetry.

四个月后的 7 月 28 日，他发现自己在同一个注册办公室，同一张表格前，他现在要为即将到来的整个学年填写该表。这一次他确切地知道他需要什么，并且他胃口是巨大的。对于注册负责人来说这胃口是太大了，注册官反对表格里他所要求的一半以上的课程，很可能是由于课程时间上的冲突。我们可以想象一位热血沸腾的中国学生和一位头脑冷静的英国注册官之间的激烈讨论，注册官划去他打算修的古英语，英语史，英国文学，英语语法和口语英语语法等课程。学生得满足于修英语语音的全课程，那已经是五门课，该领域的科研，又是两门课，一个对话课，还有，为什么不呢，埃及学的一门课，还有象形文字和符号起源课。米歇尔·霍克斯从这所高校的档案中挖掘出的一页纸的注册文件，使我们得以见证半农 1920 年 7 月底在英国首府时的心态。

刘复，当他在文件上齐整地签名时，出人意料地加了一年的年龄，他在赶时间，同时间赛跑，或者他感觉是如此吧。他担心自己的项目进度远远落后于计划，他的项目不亚于将语音科学带到中国。他认为，这门还很年轻的科学将是语言的现代研究之关键，比传统语言学更好。这就是计划。纳入计

Four months later, on July 28, he finds himself in the same registration office, in front of the same form, now to be filled out for the approaching whole new school year. This time he knows exactly what he needs, and his appetite is huge. Too huge for the officer, who is opposed to more than half of the classes requested by the student, probably because of conflicts of schedule. We imagine a heated discussion between the sanguine Chinese student and the phlegmatic British registrar, who crosses out the classes of Old English, History of English, English Literature, English Grammar, and Grammar of Colloquial English. The student must content himself with a Full Course of English Phonetics, five classes, Research Work in this field, two classes, a Conversation Class, and, why not, a course in Egyptology, Hieroglyphics and the Origin of Signs. This one-page document, Michel Hockx dug up in the archives of the institution, is telling testimony to Bannong's state of mind in the British capital at the end of July 1920.

Liu Fu, as he neatly signs the document, surprisingly adding a year to his age, is in a hurry, in a race against time, or so he feels. He fears he is way behind schedule in his project, which is nothing less than bringing to China the science of phonetics; this still young science will be the key to a modern study of the language, he believes, better than traditional linguistics. That is the plan. Incorporated in it is the idea that he himself will earn a

划的还有他的想法，就是他本人将从一个著名学府获得语言学博士学位，要知道，他甚至还没有高中文凭呢，曾被某些同事冷眼相看。但首先他得学习该学科的工具，因此他需要学习英语和英语语音，然后他才构想甚至汉语的语音。即使一个团队也要花一生的时间去做。半农只有一个人，已经三十岁了。幸运的是，他有十个人的精力、纪律和雄心壮志。他从不怀疑。然而，障碍是存在的。那位注册办公室里不合作的英国人只是其中之一，又回避不了他[5]。还有更多呢。钱，也是其中之一。伦敦吸金的程度会超出你想象。国内的政治和行政混乱导致他大学方面的津贴不再准时到达。他的积蓄象阳光下的积雪一样迅速变少。他必须花得更少。布里克斯顿距市中心很远，伦敦地铁每次收费 50 便士；另一方面，双层车又太慢，半农不是一个在公交车站等车的人。于是，他一大早就出门，步行五英里，很晚再步行回来，是英国天气里的又一个五英里。他不给自己花一毛钱。他省去早餐，略过午餐。这不会让他看上去健康的。还有更不好的。他的妻子虽没病，但是怀孕了，很虚弱。她应该去看医生（但她怎么都不去）。他们的女儿十分可爱，可他几乎忙得见不着她。她该去幼稚园了，可这不是免费的。她的衣服和鞋子小了，没钱买新的，她的妈

doctorate in linguistics, from a reputed university, he who has not even a high school diploma and is looked down upon by his colleagues. But first he has to learn the implements of the discipline, and therefore he needs to study English, *and* the phonetics of English, before he can even conceive the phonetics of Chinese. It is the work of a lifetime for a team of workers. Bannong is alone and already thirty. Fortunately, he has the energy and the discipline and the ambition of ten. He never doubts. Nevertheless, there are obstacles. The phlegmatic Brit in the office is only one of them and cannot be unseated [5]. There are more. Money, between others. London absorbs more of it than a man can believe. The stipend from his university begins not to arrive anymore, due to the political and administrative chaos in his country. His savings shrink as snow in the sun. He must spend less. Brixton is far from the city center and the London Underground is fifty pence per ride; on the other side, the double-deckers are too slow, Bannong is not a man to wait at a bus stop. So, he walks early in the morning, five miles, he walks late in the evening, five miles in the English weather. He will not spend a dime for himself. He abridges his breakfast and skips his lunch. It does not make him look healthy. There is worse. His wife is not sick but pregnant, and very weak; she should see a doctor (but protests with all her might). Their girl is adorable, but he hardly ever sees her. She should go to kindergarten, which is not free. She grows out of her

妈就织织缝缝、剪剪补补，但是还能穿多久呢？他自己的鞋子和衣服也穿旧了，他甚至不理发，在这个繁华的都市里，他看上去像个流浪汉。狄更斯出现在他的脑海里：光鲜表面下的伦敦；这位小说家一直是多么现实啊！作家能做什么来挣一些先令？他写作：为中国报纸和杂志写一些文章和故事；根据合同，他可以得到报酬，可他辛苦挣的硬币也来不到。他的课程所要求的教科书开销很大，所有书籍都要花钱，还有官僚机构每走一步和加盖印章等的费用。他的白天充满了学习，他需要用夜晚来写作，但电费是异常昂贵的，他宁可冒着看坏眼睛也用蜡烛和煤气灯。即使白天，阳光也照不到公寓。刘复努力着。他学着，但是他认为他应该学得更多。他好似面对着一堵高砖墙。

可刘复从不抱怨。如果生活艰难，几乎超出人所能承受，刘复接受它因为他是个为自己国家而战的士兵。他这种信念从没减弱过，而只是更增强他的士气。他拉直了背，你永远也听不到他的牢骚。他对未来有信心，并鼓励虚弱的国人永远不要绝望，就像他的祖先们同太平军的浴血奋战一样（他的类比！）。半农将他的脸转向光明的一面。他经常在世界上最好的大英图书馆工作，在大穹顶下，一个

clothes and shoes, there is no money to buy new, and her mother knits and stitches and cuts and patches, but for how long? His own shoes and clothes wear out too, he never even has a haircut, he begins to look like a bum in this bustling city. Dickens comes to his mind: London behind the shiny surface; how realistic the novelist had been! What can a writer do to earn some shillings? He writes: articles and stories for Chinese newspapers and magazines; and he is paid, according to the contract, but the hard coins don't arrive either. Mandatory textbooks cost a lot, all books cost, so do the fees for every step and stamp in a bureaucracy. His days are full of study, he needs his nights to write, but electricity is strangely expensive, he prefers to ruin his eyes with candles or a gaslight. Even in the day the sun avoids the apartment. Liu Fu struggles. He studies, but he should study more. He is up against a brick wall.

But Liu Fu never complains. If life is hard, almost more than one can bear, it is because he is a soldier in a fight for his country. That belief never weakens and strengthens his morale. He straightens his back and you'll never hear him whine. He has faith in the future, and he encourages weaker countrymen never to despair, like his ancestors in their desperate fight against the Taiping (his comparison!). Bannong turns his face to the bright side. He often works in the British Library, the best one of the world, under the great dome, a most awe-inspiring place,

庄重森然的地方,他喜爱这里,他知道并自豪地坐在同一张木桌前,这儿是卡尔·马克思、弗拉基米尔·列宁、孙中山等人当他们远离自己的国家,为人类的未来奋斗时曾经坐过的地方;或者像阿瑟·柯南·道尔爵士,他曾翻译并效仿的人;或者像奥斯卡·王尔德,他的朋友陈独秀钦佩的人,陈愈加钦佩因为他自己也被无辜地送进了监狱。但在图书馆,在这里和在任何地方一样,他有一个额外的职责:他已答应了他的校长他将对图书馆的目录系统进行研究,于是他尽心尽力。他写了一篇文章来帮助图书馆的李大钊,李不久将成为中国第一位马克思主义者,他的确将半农的具体建议运用到北京大学图书馆的新目录编排中。这一文章后来在《北京大学日刊》上连载发表,全国其他主要的图书馆也因此获益颇多。感谢于异国他乡的前线士兵,祖国确实取得了进步。

我们,这个放括号里说,很惊讶地看到,在 1920 年那时虽然还没有航空邮件,欧洲与中国之间的交流情况有多么好。因此我们的诗人生活在伦敦,他的半个心可以在中国,情感上同他江阴的家相连接,事业上同他北京的工作相连接。因此他从朋友那里听到他早些时候开了头的讨论如何在这个春天又爆发的消息。总而言之,这是关于中文里缺少一

he loves it, aware and proud of sitting at the same wooden tables as Karl Marx, Vladimir Lenin, Sun Yat-sen, when far from their country, they fought for the future of humanity; or as Sir Arthur Conan Doyle, he translated and imitated, or Oscar Wilde, his friend Chen Duxiu admired, the more so since he was sent to prison, innocently, too. But in the library, here as everywhere, he has a supplementary duty: he has promised his President to make a study of the library catalog system, and he studies it with care. He writes a paper, for the benefit of Li Dazhao, soon to be the first Chinese Marxist, who will indeed apply Bannong's precise proposal to the new catalog of the Peking University Library, he is the librarian of. The paper will be published as a series in the Peking University Daily; and other major libraries all over China will take advantage of it. The country does make progress thanks to her vanguard soldier in the foreign land.

We are, this said between parentheses, surprised to see how well communication functioned between Europe and China in 1920, before airmail existed. Thanks to this, our poet lives in London, but half of his heart can be in China, sentimentally in his family home in Jiangyin, and professionally with his work in Beijing. And so, he hears from friends how a discussion he had started himself flares up this spring. It regards, to summarize a long

个女性代词，缺少一个"她"字的事情[6]。半农曾在同事圈子里提出了"他"的女性变体，不同的作者开始试用这个字。周作人曾将半农的这一观点公之于众，某位寒冰，半农不认识，正在写一系列的反对该观点的文章。辩论是严肃激烈的，而且持续了好几个月，争论从完全不需要这样的代词发展到（在白话文本的写作中）绝对必要。鲁迅，周作人，还有半农最好的朋友钱玄同等多数知识分子确实捍卫了"伊"这个字，听上去不同于男性的"他"。胡适提议了一个四字序列"那个女人"（多么优雅！像绑定的脚！）。当寒冰第二次攻击时，半农反击了。在6月6日一篇强有力的辩论文章《她字问题》中，半农解释了他的选择"她"[7]是如何方便，此字（同他相比）没有语音上的偏离，易读，书面也易于识别，并有历史先例和早期实践的备注；"伊"字遭遇的问题是它太新同时又太经典；历史表明他是对的；尽管时常发生的戏剧性的争议要等十年才告结束，中国社会选择了半农的"她"。半农坚定不移。不幸的是，这份在他看来确凿的、至少对中国人口中的女性部分有着历史分量的文章，已经寄去数周了还没登出来。

story, the lack in Chinese of a feminine pronoun, a character for "she", or "her" [6]. Bannong had in the private circle of friends and colleagues proposed a female variant of "he" or "him" (*ta*), such as various authors started practicing it. Zhou Zuoren had made this opinion public, and a certain Han Bing, unknown to Bannong, was writing a series of articles against it. The debate was serious, heated, and lasted several months, the arguments going from no need at all for such a pronoun to great necessity of it (in the case of the writing of *baihua* text). Lu Xun, Zhou Zuoren, and even Bannong's best friend Qian Xuantong, indeed most intellectuals defended a character *yi*, visibly *and* audibly differing from masculine *ta*. Hu Shi proposed a sequence of four characters (How elegant! Like bound feet!). When Han Bing charges a second time, Bannong counterattacks. In a strong polemical article, "On the Issue of the Character Ta", finished June 6, he explains how his choice, *(:ta,* (她) [7] is the convenient one *because* it is not deviating from actual use in speech, it is easy to read and to recognize in writing, and it is backed by historical precedent and beginning practice. *Yi* would suffer from being too new and too classical at the time. History has shown Bannong right; although it would take a decade before the often dramatic controversy was over, the Chinese people has chosen for *(:ta.* Bannong didn't doubt. Unfortunately however, his paper, conclusive in his eyes, of historic weight at least for the

这种拖延很可能加剧了半农的紧张情绪，紧迫感和从中国缺席的痛苦，这些继而转化为他幻想他将会修的新学年课程清单。是 7 月 28 日那天吗，他发着烧回到家？他一定病得不轻，因为他没有阻止朱惠和已经能说些英语的小惠半夜去敲邻居家的门，询问医生的地址。这好像是他们第一次同住在隔壁的邻居联系！医生和邻居在一个阴郁的公寓里发现一个生病瘦弱的父亲，一个辛苦虚弱的、临近分娩的母亲，和一个苍白的四岁大的孩子。

半农的发烧证明是个好运。朱惠能够被匆忙地送往医院。若在当时的中国这种情况可能不会发生，她已经两次失去早产儿，我们高兴的是她在 8 月 1 日因剖腹产而得救。英格兰也有好的方面。剖腹产也挽救了她的双胞胎，很小的一个女孩和很小的一个男孩，他们被暂时留在重症监护室。新生儿得到的名字跟当时的环境相对应：育伦和育敦，他们一起在伦敦成长。

female part of the Chinese population, had been mailed since weeks, but had not appeared yet.

The delay may well have added to Bannong's nervousness, feeling of urgency and the painful absence from China, embodied into his shopping list of courses he fancied he could take in the new school year. Was it that day, July 28, that he came home with a fever? He must have fallen ill seriously, because he didn't prevent Zhu Hui and little Xiao Hui, who spoke some English already, from knocking on the neighbor's door in the middle of the night and asking for the address of a doctor. It seems to have been the first time they connected with the people living next door! Doctor and neighbors discover in the somber apartment an ill and meager father, a suffering weak mother, pregnant to her teeth, and a pale four-year-old child.

Bannong's fever proved of good fortune. Zhu Hui was in a rush taken to the hospital. This would not have happened in China, where she had twice lost a premature child, and we rejoice, because she was saved by a cesarean intervention on the first of August. In some way, England was good. The cesarean saved also the twins she gave birth to. A very little girl and a very little boy, sent into intensive care for the time being. The newborns would get names responding to the circumstances: *Yulun* and *Yudun*, together *Bring up in London*.

读者自己可以想象一下刘半农的感受。

八月是在家和医院之间度过的,也是在幸福感和沉重的焦虑感之间度过的。如何支付医院费用?如何支付房租?没有一分余钱。朱惠已精疲力竭,在危及生命的分娩手术后她需要时间来找回她最低限度的力量。日常的家务琐事,在这种情况下更是加倍了,都得靠父亲(和他可爱的女儿)。夜晚休息不成,正如所有年轻父亲经验中体会到的那样。对近期前景的担忧越来越多。如何喂养多出来的两张嘴?如何设计五个人的住所?母亲还在康复中,他怎样花时间在学校?同两个哭闹的婴儿一起,晚上怎样写作? 八月过去了。九月开始了。

不管谁第一次读《教我如何不想她》都可以很容易地想象出一位诗人,手里拿支笔,迎风坐在海边的石头或草地上,看着水和天空,直到夜幕降临,诗人任凭他的思绪随着风和海水远行,禁不住比照他在国外的现实和他遥远的家乡。如果我们细心想一下,这情景是不可能的。当现在我们知道较多的情况,问题也来了。

这首诗是什么时候写的,在哪里写的?签的日期是1920年9月4日。就从这儿开始吧,这是我们

Readers can imagine Liu Bannong's feelings all by themselves.

The month of August passed between home and hospital, between happiness and heavy concern. How to pay for the hospital? How to pay the rent? There was no penny left. Zhu Hui was exhausted; she needed time to find a minimum of strength back after the life-threatening childbirth surgery. Daily chores, doubled by the circumstances, were all for the father (and his adorable daughter). The nights were of no rest, as all young fathers know from experience. The concerns for the immediate future piled up. How to feed two more mouths? How to organize the apartment for five? How to spend time at the university when the mother was still in recovery? How to write at night with two crying babies? The month of August passed. September began.

Whoever reads *How can I not miss her?* for the first time, imagines easily a poet, a pen in his hand, sitting on a windy day at the border of the ocean on a stone or in the grass, watching the water and the sky until the fall of night, letting his thoughts travel with the wind and the sea, riding on the contrast between his foreign reality and his faraway homeland. A more attentive look makes this improbable. Now we know more of the circumstances, questions rise.

When was it written and where? It was signed September 4, 1920. Let us start there; it is the only thing

唯一知道的。 1920年9月4日是星期六。学校很快就要开学了，半农还没开始上课。他有空，这是新学年之前最后的自由日子。他是呆在家里吗？两个婴儿只有一个月大，他的妻子还在康复中。或是他第一次出门，因为母婴都已从医院回来？他是否感到些愉快能逃离片刻，找回他的老节奏？就他的学习和写作而言，这整个八月是失去了。最终除了一些诗歌。他可能像以往自由时候一样去了大英图书馆。他就会步行过去，那是一个夏日的周六。他可能看到的唯一重要的水（不排除雨水，那天的天气该是多变的）就是泰晤士河，他要经滑铁卢桥穿过这条河，那是通往图书馆的最短途径。这条河宽阔浩瀚，但谁会称它为海洋呢？一个人可以站在桥的中央，惊叹于河岸和船只。他也可以在傍晚经同一座桥回来，但月亮会爱上泰晤士河吗？他也可以在公园里停留，路上有几处，比如维多利亚堤岸花园，他可以坐在长凳上，很诗意。半农不是一个梦想者，他是一个工作者，而他本可以破一次例的。

  我可以继续猜测，但只有一件事似乎是肯定的，半农那天不在海边。他在伦敦，在高大的图书馆里，或者在他家低低的天花板下某个暗暗的房间里。他

we know. September 4, 1920 was a Saturday. School was to start soon; Bannong had not yet classes that day. He was free, his last free day before a new year. Did he stay home? The babies were only a month old and his wife was still recovering. Or did he go out for the first time since mother and babies had returned from the hospital? Was he happy to escape, to find his old ways back? The whole month of August was, in terms of his study and writing, a lost month, apart from some poetry, eventually. He might have gone to the British Library, as he often did on free days. He would have walked, it was a summer Saturday. The only water (save some rain, the weather being very changeable that day) of any importance he could have seen, was the Thames, when he crossed it over the Waterloo Bridge, the shortest way to the library. The river is wide and mighty, but who would call it the ocean? One can stop in the middle of a bridge and marvel at the shores and the ships. He could have returned by the same bridge in the evening, but would the moon fall in love with the Thames? He could have stopped at a park, there were several on his road, like the Victoria Embankment Gardens, and sit on a bench, very poetic. Bannong was not a dreamer, rather a worker, but he could have made an exception.

I could continue guessing, but only one thing seems sure, Bannong was not at the ocean that day. He was in London, in the lofty Library or at home in a dark room

有自由，他的自由是写一首诗；或者完成他几周前已经开始的那首。我们发现这首诗不存在时间或地点的统一。某个夜晚，我们发现自己同水中月亮的倒影在一起，另一个场景是枯萎的树木映衬在天空炽红的落日里，又一个是我们同诗人漫步在清新的微风里。一时天气寒冷，一时清凉宜人。我们不得不得出结论：诗人试图用言语捕捉的不是他用眼睛可以看到的东西：他的眼睛是闭着的，图像跳到他的脑海里，就像回忆起卷轴上的图画。四幅画，它们是四个季节的画面，以适当的顺序出现：清新微风的春天，银光闪闪的夏日，燕子离去的秋天，鲜明日落的冬天。类似地，虽然以更随机的顺序，我们可以发现一天中的不同时间：多云的早晨，空气停滞的夜晚和满月，慵懒的下午以及一天的尾声。季节或一天中的各个时辰是生命周期（时间）和宇宙或世界（空间）的象征，空间更被空气、水、地球和火等元素的不可否认的存在所强化了。这些混合了欧亚谱系的图像，你若在布里克斯顿或布卢姆斯伯里去寻找的话，将是徒劳的，它们是来自远方的图像，来自中国的，很可能是江苏的，印在心上的图像。具有普遍的吸引力。他们住在心灵的眼睛里，在那里诗人不由自主地看到他们，给他们命名，凝视他们。他们把诗人带到母亲祖国。相对于常被

under a low ceiling. He was free, and his freedom was to write a poem; or finish one he had started in the last weeks. In this poem, we observe now no unity of time or place. At one time at night we find ourselves with the reflection of the moon in the water; at another in a landscape with withered trees, seen against the sky where the sun sets in fiery red; at still another we walk with the poet in a fresh breeze. Now it is bitter cold, now pleasantly cool. We must conclude: What the poet tries to capture in words is not something he sees with his eyes: his eyes are closed, and images pop up in his mind, like the remembrance of paintings on scrolls. Four paintings, they are, of the four seasons, in due order: fresh windy spring, silver light summer, autumn when the swallow leaves us, winter with a dramatic sunset. Similarly, though in more random order, we may find the hours of the day: cloudy morning, airless night and full moon, lazy afternoon, and the end of day. The seasons, or the hours of the day, are symbols of the life cycle (time) and of the universe or world (space), reinforced by the undeniable presence of the elements: air, water, earth and fire. These images, of mixed European and Asian pedigree, one would in vain look for in Brixton or Bloomsbury, they are pictures from far, pictures of China, of Jiangsu Province possibly, images of the mind. Of universal appeal. And they dwell in the mind's eye, where the poet can't help seeing them, naming them, contemplating them; they bring him to the motherland.

很快解读成的"我多么想念她!",这首诗的语气和意义显然更加微妙:不是现在的伦敦、英国或大西洋的画面使他思虑万千而痛惜与中国的距离,而是一种恒定心态的各种憧憬。不是(苛刻的)现实与(甜蜜的)记忆之间的反差,而是承认永久记忆的情怀;与其说是渴望不如说是归属于"她"。最后,不是抱怨,而是意识到那无条件的爱。诗人,在一种极端的状况下闭上了他的眼睛,呼唤她,看见她,他的"视觉"使他爱她,想念她;并使他克服绝望,因为这种爱就是为什么他在他所在的地方,就像战壕里的士兵一样,穷困而坚定。

这些正是刘半农需要的鼓舞人心的话,某个时刻他似乎已跌到了谷底。他需要把他的士气高昂的言语作为一首诗写下来,当疑虑想要入侵他的内心,他可以借此激励自己。这一次他创作了一首极其个人的诗。

她是谁?我们可以给她一个名字吗?我们当然有选择。在整整一个月的时间里,在生活所能提供的最令人情绪化的情形,半农一直和妻子在一起。她本来很可能那么轻易地死去,但相反她却给了新的生命。同时,诗人和女儿的亲情更深了,女儿经

The poem, often (too hurriedly) read as *"How do I miss her!"*, is more subtle in tone and in meaning than that: not images of present London or England or the Atlantic obliging his thoughts to melancholically deplore the distance to China, but the various visions of a constant state of mind; not a contrast between (harsh) reality and (sweet) memories, but the acknowledgment of permanent recollections; not *longing* as much as *belonging*, to "her". Finally, not a complaint, but the recognition of unconditional love. The poet, in a desperate situation, closing his eyes, calls for *her*, sees *her*, and his "visions" make him love *her*, miss *her*; and make him overcome his despair, because this love is why he is where he is, like a soldier in a trench, destitute but determined.

Those were the words of courage Liu Bannong needed to hear, at a moment he seemed to hit the bottom. Words of his ever-high morale, he needed to write them down as a poem, to motivate himself, when doubts threatened to break into his heart. And this time, contrary to habits, he composed a most personal poem.

Who is *she?* Can we give her a name? We certainly have choices. During a whole month, Bannong has been with his wife in the most emotional circumstances life can offer. She could have died so easily, but she had given new life instead. At the same time, he has strengthened the bond with his daughter, who had experienced the

历了弟弟和妹妹的出生，人们常常注意到这时候女儿自然而然地会同父亲更亲近。他的爱情民谣的想法很可能是因为伦敦孤独中他的两个忠实的女性伴侣。小惠似乎引用了中国的说法："月惟故乡明。"这首诗的视野立刻开阔了。他的家在江阴，那里有他深爱的弟弟、弟媳。从那里到国家仅一步之遥，祖国母亲，她就是他远去的原因，她处于极大的危险中。她会活到复兴，即重生吗？这与他个人情况的类比太显著了，因此不能被忽视。

既然我说到绘画，就像脑海里可以看到的四卷轴，悬挂于墙上，慢慢从下读到上空，或者耐心地在桌子上展开，它们是由诗人以最清晰、古典和简洁的风格绘出的。一些著名作品出现在脑海里，如明代画家沈周的《中秋望月图》，清代画家八大山人的《鱼石图》，或宋代画家梁楷所绘的著名诗人李白的假想画像《太白行吟图》。刘半农是知道自己的意图的：他想表明，用简单的口语词汇，用白话，就像用最少的笔触绘画一样，一个人可以写出像古典诗句一样完美的诗句，一样有规律性和对称性的、一样轻盈而亲密的、一样真实而直接的、却又一样练达的。你可以写一首民歌，比如英语民谣，

birth of siblings; in a natural way, often observed, she had grown closer to her father. The idea of his love ballad may well have risen because of his two faithful female partners in his London loneliness. Xiao Hui seems to have quoted the Chinese saying that the "moon shines nowhere brighter than at home". Immediately the horizon of Bannong's poem widens. His home is in Jiangyin with his brothers and sisters-in-law he deeply loves. From there it is only one step to the country itself, the nation, and *she* is the reason why he is far, *she* is in great danger. Will *she* live up to a renaissance, a rebirth? The analogies with his personal situation are too evident to be overlooked.

Since I said paintings, like mentally visible on four scrolls, hanging on a wall and slowly read from the bottom to the sky, or rolled out patiently on a table, they are brushed by the poet in the most clear, classical and economic style. Famous works come to mind on their side, like *Watching the Moon,* by the Ming painter Shen Chou, *Fish and Rocks* by Qing painter Bada Shanren, or the well-known imaginary portrait of poet Li Po, by Song Dynasty painter Liang Kai. Liu Bannong's intention is conscious: he wants to show that with simple colloquial words, in *baihua*, like with minimal brushstrokes in painting, one can write verse as perfect as classical verse, as regular and symmetric, as light and intimate, as real and direct, and yet as sophisticated. One can write a folksong, like

触动每个男女的心。白话的反对者错误地否认这一点，他们只是将白话比作是驴子的嗯昂或牛的哞哞。

  刘半农四次强调这一点。四次他的中国场景都趋向于他的表达对母亲祖国和她的语言的热爱。对于诗人来说，《教我如何不想她》是一个成功应用的简单民谣格式。可一百年以后，我意识到这其中有多少的含义啊，现实太庞大了以致于一个人看不见，或者说以至于我们的诗人无法使之合理化，但他却在不知不觉地活出来。我必须外推和解释他所人格化否则即无法言说的东西；他只能战斗将白话变成诗歌。一个世纪之后，那种战斗对我们来说几乎不再鲜活了。一个世纪之后，我们不禁想看得更远。在这些天真无邪的线条下面，中国发生了更大范围的生存和文化转变，而诗中著名的副歌则为我们提供了一个窥视孔，让我们得到一个直接的视图。一个本地的儿子在言说。他的祖国母亲永远在他的心上。要是帝国的话，祖国父亲一词就会是适当的语言。但现在他已成为共和国的臣民，那是他过去所有的愿望。共和国的形象是一个女人。想想法国！但不是处女，不是情妇，而是母亲。这是白话的必然结果。白话是母语。你与人民的关系正在从父性转变到母性。人们对家国的感情正在加深，少了些抽象，多了些实体，少了些严苛，多了些温柔，少

an English ballad, speaking to every man and woman. The adversaries of *baihua* are mistaken in denying that, when they compare the vernacular to the braying of the ass or the mooing of the cow.

Four times Liu Bannong underscores it. Four times his Chinese landscape scenes tend to a declaration of love for the motherland and her language. *How could I not miss her?* For the poet it was a simple ballad formula successfully applied. One hundred years later, I realize how much more was implied, a reality too huge for a man to see or for our poet to rationalize, but one he unconsciously *lived*. I must extrapolate and interpret what he personified but could not verbalize otherwise than as his struggle to turn *baihua* into poetry. That struggle is hardly alive to us, a century hence. A century hence, we can't help but look beyond it. A much vaster existential and cultural shift happens in China under the surface of these innocent lines, and the famous refrain opens a peephole through which we get a direct view. A native son is speaking. His motherland is permanently on his mind. If it had been the Empire, the word fatherland would have been proper language. But now he is the citizen of a Republic. The image of it is a woman. Think of France! But not a virgin, not a mistress, a mother. This is the inevitable consequence of *baihua*. Which is the mother tongue. Relations to the people are changing from paternal to maternal. Feelings about the nation are deepening, becoming less abstract, more corporeal, less

了些冷淡。我们现在最好用一个孩子仰望母亲的方式来描述这些感情。母爱和孩子对母爱的回应是多么非同寻常啊！多么美好的关系！半农当然每一天每一个小时都能看见这种关系。他的诗心怎能不被感动？难道不该吗？在整个八月期间，他没看到、没听到、没触摸过任何别的东西。他怎么可能会错过写它呢？孩子多么脆弱，母亲多么勇敢，他们之间的相互吸引是多么自然，还有，他们的处境是多么危险。到头来它是多么神秘。爱的神密就是生命的神密。

  唉！他的语言缺乏这个词来表达这种基本的身体状态，这是大自然教的、所有人都有的最深层的情感：一个孩子对"她"的爱。诗人的语言区分不开帝国和共和国，区分不开他和她。只能呼唤他，对她却一言不发。这需要修复：所有革命中最小的，但最重要的一次。他的父权制古典语言必须接受剖腹产手术。如果不的话，诗歌将会死掉。语言必须为更母性，更自然的白话创造空间，一个独立的字----"她"就是白话的象征。创造这个字是诗人的无与伦比的职责。从字的所有意义来构想它。一首诗必

strict, more tender, less cold. We can best describe them now in terms of a child looking up to the mother. How extraordinary is motherly love, and the child's response! How overwhelming the relationship! Bannong, of course, sees it before him every day, every hour of the day. Could his poetic soul not be touched? Should it not? During the whole month of August, he has seen nothing else, heard, touched nothing else. How could he miss writing about it? How fragile the child, how courageous the mother, how natural their mutual attraction, also how perilous their condition. How mysterious in the end. The mystery of love is the mystery of life.

Alas! His language lacks the word to express this fundamental physical condition, this deepest of all emotions, taught by nature, shared by all humans: the love of a child for *her*. His language cannot distinguish between the Empire and the Republic, between him and her; it can only call on him, has no word for her. This needs repair: though the smallest of all revolutions, it is one of the most significant. His patriarchal classical language must undergo a cesarean intervention; if not poetry will die. It must make place for the more maternal, the more natural *baihua*, the symbol of which will be an independent word for *her*. It is the duty, *par excellence,* of the poet to invent that word. To *conceive it,* in all the senses of the word. A poem must introduce

须将这个字介绍到言语中，通过用它、重复它，必要时重复它四次给聋子的耳朵，最终即使聋子耳朵也会接收到。不是抱怨，而是祈祷。不是绝望，而是神秘地传达着希望、信念和爱，这是只有孩子在不知不觉中才能够提供的。

8月1日，两个孩子在英格兰出生，一个男孩，一个女孩。

8月9日，半农关于"她"的文章发表在上海的《时事新报》。

刘氏夫妇可以区分双胞胎，中国可以区分男人和女人。在诗人的怀里一首诗正在成熟，在充满威胁的沮丧中，希望的信息结晶在这个新字中。

刘复为此诗签的日期是九月的那个周六。他没有想那么多：用口语语言愉快地玩耍，并故意使用"她"，在经过数周的生活压力后他正慢慢地好起来。这对于一天来说已经足够好了。他的注意力集中在诗意质量上，而不在于意义的层次。以后别的人会为他做这些，他没去想，然后他把诗放在一边。他没有把诗寄给《新青年》，那里他的一些同事会认为它很肤浅或简单。与他平时的习惯相反，他没有发表。我们不要忘了他先是在英国，接下来的几年是在法国。也许他觉得这首诗太个人了，直到

it into speech, by using it, by repeating it, if need be, four times for deaf ears, who will eventually pick it up. Not a complaint, but a prayer; not despair, but mysteriously a message of hope, faith and love, as only a child, unconsciously, can offer.

On August 1, two children were born in England, a boy and a girl.

On August 9, Bannong's article on *(:ta* was published in the Shanghai newspaper China Times.

She was born to China. The Liu's could differentiate between the twins, China between man and woman. And in the poet's bosom a poem was ripening, in which, out of threatening frustration, the message of hope was crystallized in this one new word.

Liu Fu dated the poem on that Saturday in September. He didn't think that much of it: a pleasant play with colloquial language and the deliberate use of *(:ta*, welling up after weeks of stress. That was good enough for the day. His attention had focused on the poetic qualities, not on the layers of its meaning. That others would do this later for him, he did not imagine, and he put the poem away. He did not send it to *New Youth*, where some of his colleagues could have considered it shallow or facile. Contrary to his habits, he did not publish it. Let us not forget that he lived now in England, the following years in France. Maybe he felt it was too personal. He waited with the publication until September 16, 1923, in

1923年9月16日，他才在《北京晨报》副刊上发表[8]，此诗有一个朴实的标题《情歌》，署名刘复。他很可能以前已和朋友们分享过，出乎预料的是，它很快在文学圈广为人知。很可能是当它在赵元任的手中变成歌曲的时候，它得到了现有的标题[9]。文字和音调结合起来的活力征服了全国的心灵，这超出了半农的梦想，但没有超出他的愿望。与民族的交融是他的生活。他是情不自禁的，这体现在他所做的一切里。这首诗因此不是从伦敦的天上掉下来的。它的妊娠已经超过一天了。诗和诗人对女性代词的专注有机地交织在一起。他十二年来翻译充满对话的英语文本的习惯，让他确信她的绝对必要性，跟"他"一起，但能区分开来的"她"，以增加行文流畅和防止奇怪的误解。当诗人在北京寻找正确的字时，那是"她"的胚胎期。孕期对应于他让她靠近自己的心，防御来自保守派作家和不太友好的进步作家的敌对势力。伦敦的日常英语活动最终使这种中文的更新对他来说成为当务之急，诗人

the Beijing Morning News Supplement [8]. Its unpretentious title was "A Love Song", signed Liu Fu. He had probably shared it with friends before. Against the odds, it was quickly well-known in literary circles. It received its current title probably when it became a song in the hands of Zhao Yuanren [9]. The combined vitality of words and tones conquered the soul of the Chinese people. It was more than Bannong had dreamed of, not more than he had wished. This communion with the nation was what he lived for. Quite literally, he could not help thinking of it in all he did. The poem, therefore, did not fall from the London sky. Its gestation had taken more than one day. It was organically interwoven with his preoccupation with a feminine pronoun. His twelve-year habit of translating English texts, full of dialogue, had convinced him of the absolute necessity of *(:ta* (她)*,* next to but differentiated from masculine *ta* (他)*,* in order to add fluency to texts and prevent odd misunderstandings. We situate the embryonic phase of the new pronoun in Beijing, when Bannong had searched for the correct characters, weighed them and found *(:ta* the best candidate. The pregnancy period corresponds to his keeping *her* close to his heart, against the cold headwinds coming from conservative authors and not-so-Bannong-friendly progressive writers. The everyday practice of English in London, finally, made this "update" of Chinese imperative for him, this update for his

要朝着现代世界更新他的语言,在现代世界中,妇女争取与男子平等,在现代世界中,女孩和男孩该有同样的机会,像双胞胎。不管什么季节、什么时辰,当她出生时,他怎能不考虑她?他怎能不写一首小诗赋予"她"生命?在适度平衡下,一个用美和爱定义的生命。正是半农的诗的天赋,在它最坦诚的时刻,将他多年的复杂经历凝聚成一些简单的行和平衡的语气,"她"正好走进每一个中国公民的心里。

杨·劳伦斯·西思翎
2020 年 9 月 3 日
美国哈蒂斯堡---密西西比

田海燕 译

language to the modern world, where women were fighting for equality and where girls would have the same opportunities as boys, like twins. When *she* was born as *(:ta*, how could he not think of *her*, in whatever season at whatever hour? How could he not write a little poem giving life to *her*? A life defined by beauty and love, in a just balance. It was Bannong's poetic talent in its most candid moment, that would condense years of complex experience into a few simple lines and a well-balanced tone, going right to the heart of every Chinese citizen.

Jan Laurens Siesling

September 3, 2020
Hattiesburg, Mississippi
USA

尾注

————————————————

[1] 我要感谢三个人为使得这篇文章的写作有价值而提供的帮助。对于本文中的大部分传记资料，我感谢胡美凤女士于 2019 年出版的关于刘氏兄弟的书《流风》。尽管它是用丰富的想象力构造出的家庭小说，胡女士的文献却是部分地根据存档在江阴刘氏博物馆的刘半农及兄弟的日记。本书帮助我重构了诗人在写诗时的个人情况。伦敦大学的注册表复印件是印第安纳州圣母大学的中文教授米歇尔·霍克斯（Michel Hockx）提供给我的。米歇尔撰写了关于二十世纪早期的诗人尤其是有关刘半农的书籍和文章。小提琴教授刘育熙，刘半农先生的侄子，从我对刘半农的兴趣出发，帮我查找英语资源所没有的信息。我衷心感谢田海燕，我的妻子，她对我所有中文问题的不懈回答，并将本文译成她的母语。从网络上我得到其它的一些零星信息，网上信息多有重复，且很少提及来源。

[2] 刘育熙教授向我转告了俄勒冈州波特兰孔子学院组织的一场百人翻译比赛，该比赛于 2020 年 8 月 20 日进行评审。我不是一个艺术和文学比赛的支持者，于是决定不参加。

Endnotes

---

[1] I wish to thank three people for having helped making the writing of this essay worthwhile. For much of the biographical information in this essay I am indebted to the recent book about the Liu brothers by Mrs. Hu Meifeng, "Liu Feng", published in 2019. Although with rich imagination composed as a family novel, Mrs. Hu's documentation is in part based on the notebooks of Liu Bannong and his brothers, kept in the archives of the Liu Museum in Jiangyin. It has helped me to reconstruct the personal circumstances of the poet at the moment of writing the poem. Regarding the copies of the registration forms at the London University, I received them from Michel Hockx, Professor of Chinese at the Notre Dame University, Indiana, and author of books and articles on early twentieth century poets, notably about Liu Bannong. Professor of violin Liu Yuxi, Mr. Liu Bannong's nephew, standing at the origin of my interest in Liu Bannong, reached out to find information that didn't exist in English sources. I express my infinite gratitude to Haiyan Tian, my wife and tireless responder to all questions Chinese. She translated the text to her mother tongue. Other flashes of information are found dispersed over the internet, rarely adding anything not found in the others and rarely mentioning sources.

[2] Professor Liu Yuxi communicated to me the organization by Confucius Institute of Portland, OR, of a competition between one hundred translators of the poem, to be juried on August 20, 2020. Not being a supporter of competitions in the arts and letters, I decided not to participate.

[3] 你可以将其与半农后来的同事林语堂在《苏东坡传》（1946年出版）中的捍卫包办婚姻相提并论。

[4] 在欧洲，学年通常是从9月至7月中旬，以圣诞节和复活节为间隔，分为三个学期。它解释了注册表中的异常，该表的印章日期为4月2日，但签名日期为4月27日。4月2日是复活节前的最后一个星期五。接着学校将关闭三周，半农将不得不再次回来同意并签字。另一个令人惊讶的细节是刘复填在表格上的出生日期：1890年4月20日，而不是1891年5月27日。我们将在接下来的一本有关刘氏家族的书中探索这个谜。

[5] 实际上，第二年刘半农决定去巴黎继续他的语音学深造，那里的规则很可能更适合他的个性。

[6] 黄兴涛在《"她"字的文化史》（2009，中文）一书中对此主题进行了广泛的研究。互联网上有两个有帮助的评论。

[7] 我将在英文文本中使用缩写形式（:ta 来表示"她"。

[8] 感谢刘育熙向我转发鲍晶所写的刘半农的权威传记中的相关资料。

[9] 赵元任似乎是在美国的时候偶然知道这首诗的。两个朋友于1925年在巴黎相见。

[3] You may compare this to the defense of arranged marriages by Bannong's colleague of later years, Lin Yutang, in his biography of Su Dongpo, "The Gay Genius", published in 1946.

[4] In Europe the school year would typically run from September to mid-July, in three terms, separated by Christmas and Easter. It explains an anomaly on the registration form, which bears the stamp date of April 2, but is signed and dated April 27th. April 2nd was the last Friday before Easter. Then the school would be closed for three weeks, and Bannong would have to come back to agree and sign. Another surprising detail is the birth date Liu Fu writes in to the form: April 20, 1890, instead of May 27, 1891. We will study this riddle in a forthcoming book on the Liu family.

[5] In fact, the next year Liu Bannong decided to pursue his studies of phonetics in Paris, where the rules may well have been more adapted to his personality.

[6] An extensive study of the subject is Huang Xingtao, *A Cultural History of the Character Ta (She)*, 2009 (Chinese). There are two helpful reviews of it available on the Internet.

[7] I will use in this paper the abridged form **(:ta** for "feminine ta".

[8] With thanks to Liu Yuxi for transmitting me the relevant pages from the authoritative biography of Liu Bannong by Bao Jing, with this information.

[9] Zhao Yuanren seems to have known the poem when he was in the United States, and by accident. The two friends met in Paris in 1925.

赵元任 （1892-1982）

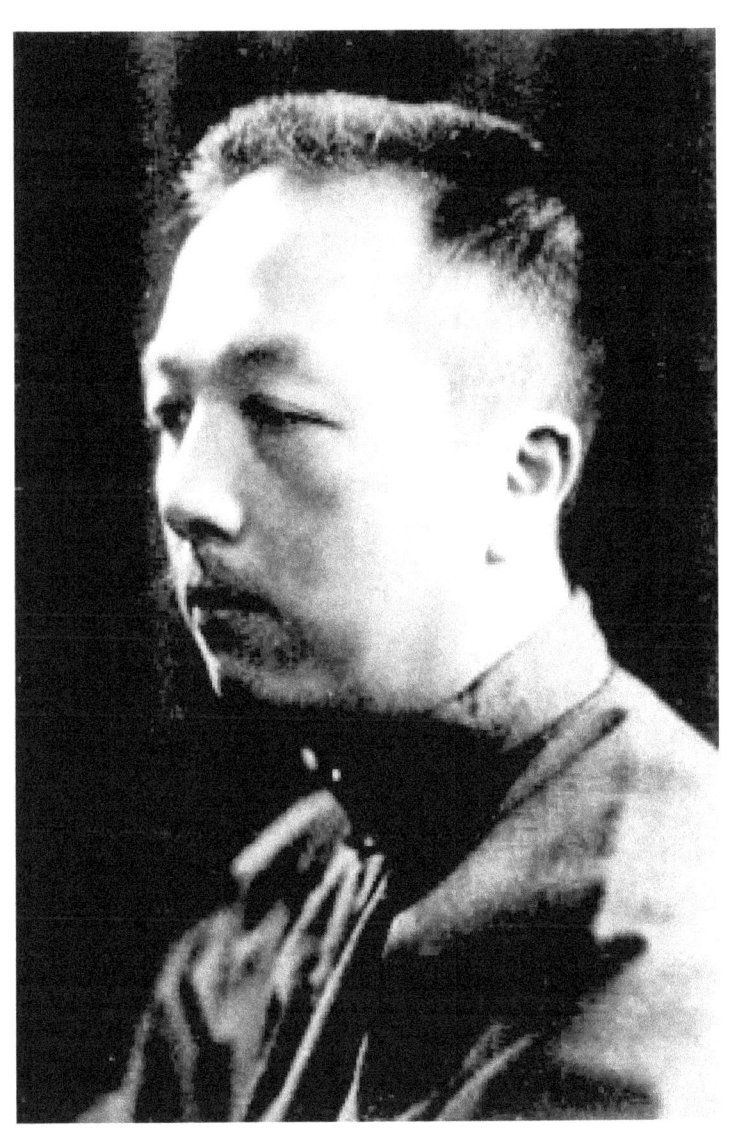

刘半农 (1891-1934)

赵元任的曲谱

1926 年，著名语言学家赵元任为刘复（刘半农）的诗《教我如何不想她》谱了曲。他当时是否发表了这个曲谱？我所找到最早的录音是 1936 年。（Youtube.com，赵元任演唱的《教我如何不想她》）。似乎是给一个广播电台录制的，由小提琴和钢琴伴奏，作曲家自己优美而非戏剧性地唱这支歌。令他深感悲伤的是他两年前刚失去了这位好友。

为了将歌谣译成英文，我听了元任的音乐，从现在起说英语的人也可以唱它了。互联网上有这首歌的好几种版本的曲谱，伴奏或无伴奏，或不同调式。我从中国曲谱网选择了一个最常见和最常分享的曲谱，是给声部和钢琴的。它是 E 大调，是赵元任演唱的调式。这里我提供一个中文版和一个英文版。（令人奇怪的是所见的中文歌词里用的是"他"；我对此已进行了更正。）不久你会在 youtube.com 上找到我唱这支歌；你可以来一起唱。

Zhao Yuanren's music scores

In 1926, Zhao Yuanren, the famous linguist, composed the music to Liu Fu's (or Liu Bannong's) poem *How Can I Not Miss Her*. Did he publish the score at that moment? The oldest recording, I have found, dates back to 1936. (Youtube.com, Zhao Yuanren 教我如何不想她). Apparently for a radio broadcast and accompanied by violin and piano, the composer sings the song himself, beautifully, not melodramatically. This was (only) two years after his friend Liu Fu died, to his great sorrow.

For my translation of the poem, I have followed Yuanren's music, so now we can sing it in English. There are several scores of the song's music available on the internet, with or without accompaniment, and in a variety of keys. I have chosen a score from qupu123.com, most frequently seen and shared on the net, for voice and piano. It is in E-Major, which is the key Zhao Yuanran performed it in. I provide here a Chinese and an English version. (Curiously the Chinese lyrics refer to a male person (他); I have corrected it for this edition.)

Soon you can find me singing it on youtube.com; you may sing along.

JLS

教我如何不想她

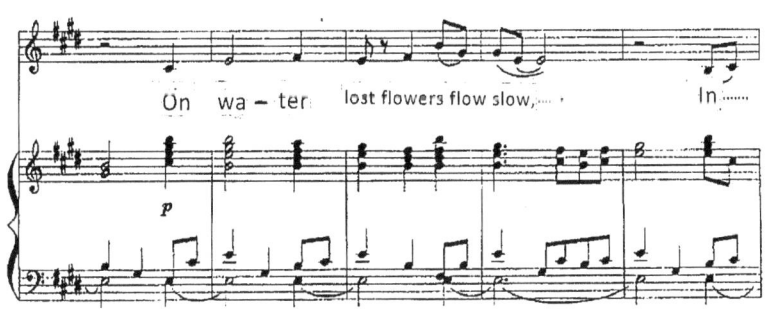

75

杨·劳伦斯·西思翎，诗人、作家、艺术史学家和译者。生于荷兰，现居于美国，曾在法国生活多年。他最近出版的书（Art is More）被译为中文《艺术不止美》，2019年由江苏凤凰美术出版社出版。他翻译的五四诗人徐玉诺的英译本诗集即将出版。

田海燕，译者。生于中国河南，居于美国，南密西西比大学数学教授。爱好艺术和诗歌，也收藏中国艺术品。

Jan Laurens Siesling is a writer of novels and poetry, art historian and translator. Born in the Netherlands, he now lives in the United States, after having lived in France for many years. A recent book *Art is More* was translated into Chinese and published by the Jiangsu Phoenix Fine Arts Publishing House in 2019. His English translation of the May 4th poet Xu Yunuo is forthcoming.

Haiyan Tian, translator. Born in Henan, China, living in the United States, she is a professor of mathematics at the University of Southern Mississippi. An amateur of art and poetry, she collects Chinese art.

Also by Jan Laurens Siesling in Just So Editions

How the Rhino Lost its Horn & Other Just So Songs
2019, poetry

Americana & One Day Jesus Christ
2020, poetry

Black Wolf or The End of a Royal House
2020, tale

By Jan Laurens Siesling with other publishers (selection)

Art is More, Arte Libro, Ghent, Belgium (also available in French, Dutch and Chinese) 2015 ….

Thierry Vernet, Peintre, Somogy, Paris, France, 2006

Le Maître de La Tour-du-Pin, Le temps qu'il fait, Cognac, France, 1988

Terence Netter, the 9/11 Series, Show catalog, 2011, Hattiesburg, MS, USA

The Spirit Between the Words, Translating Chinese Poets, Pleasure of the Text, Beijing, China, 2019

See also www.jansiesling.com & www.artismore.org

海棠诗丛